A Commonplace
Jonathan Davidson & Others

smith|doorstop

Published 2020 by
Smith|Doorstop Books
The Poetry Business
Campo House
54 Campo Lane
Sheffield S1 2EG

www.poetrybusiness.co.uk

ISBN 978-1-912196-33-3
Jonathan Davidson hereby asserts his moral right to be
identified as the author of this book.

British Library Cataloguing-in-Publication Data.
A catalogue record for this book is available from the
British Library.

Design & typeset by Tim Morris
Cover image: 'The Industrial Henge'
by Anna Dillon (www.annadillon.com).
Author photo by Lee Allen
Printed by T J International

Smith|Doorstop Books is a member of Inpress:
www.inpressbooks.co.uk. Distributed by
NBN International, 1 Deltic Avenue,
Rooksley, Milton Keynes MK13 8LD.

The Poetry Business gratefully acknowledges the support
of Arts Council England.

Contents

A Note on A Commonplace

The poems by Jonathan Davidson that feature in this collection were written between 1981 and 2019 in Didcot, Leicester, Ilkley, Skipton, Coventry, Denbighshire, Birmingham and Sheffield, and in Ventspils (Latvia) and Kyiv (Ukraine). The commentary was written in Birmingham between Summer 2018 and Summer 2019. The final edits took place during July 2019 in Haapsalu (Estonia) and from October to December 2019 in Birmingham.

For Mollie & Frederick and my Mother and late Father

Introduction

Poems – my own and other people's – are scattered across my life. They are in books and notebooks, folded in wallets and hidden in desk drawers; a few are memorised. They are as commonplace as food and drink. I wouldn't want to live without them, although I dare say I could. They will be the last things I forget when everything else is gone. Some of these poems are gathered together in this book, *A Commonplace*.

A Commonplace is a collection of my own poems interleaved with other people's poems, poems I admire and that give solace or inspiration. As there are things I want to say about my own poems, and about those by other poets, I have included an ongoing commentary. This isn't something I've done before, but it has made me think about how poetry is released into the world. By strange chance I learned, half-way through writing the commentary, that Ted Hughes had *almost* gone down the same path. Here's what he said in 1989:[1]

> '*I've been thinking of making a selection of my verses and setting them in a commentary – like the* Vita Nuova. *The pieces I mostly read. // This is heresy. But there seems to me a possibility that many poems simply slip from the great memory because they lack context.*'[2]

I'm not afraid of heresy: heresy is my middle name.[3] The commentary is the context.

Footnotes are given to some of the poems and to the commentary. They add afterthoughts and additional information. A bibliography is no bad thing for the curious reader, and so one is included.

---

1   From a letter to Keith Sagar, 5 August 1989, p. 174, *Poet and Critic: The Letters of Ted Hughes and Keith Sagar.*
2   I am indebted to my friend Greg Leadbetter for bringing this letter to my attention.
3   It's not. My middle name is Frederick.

11

There is also a gazetteer, with grid-references where locations are difficult to identify by name only. Readers can set off to visit them all and be home by Christmas.[4]

Gathered together – the poems, the commentary, the footnotes, the bibliography and the gazetteer – the whole forms a kind of commonplace book.[5] So, having now introduced *A Commonplace: Apples, Bricks & Other People's Poems*, we can begin. Here follows, overleaf, a poem I like very much by Richie McCaffery.

---

4   Which Christmas I wisely do not say. It makes quite a journey: you'll need a flask and some sandwiches.

5   Commonplace books were common from the Renaissance onwards. They were a place to gather all sorts of ideas, quotes and memories.

Brick

By Richie McCaffery

They say Belgians are born with a brick
in their stomachs, such is their love
of property. It's taken us until now
to have a few thousand of our own.

I've brought little to the buying
of this place, but I do have a brick.
It's deeply stamped *Radcliffe* –
the brickworks (that no longer exist)

that made the red blocks
of the 1930s semi I called home.
My rough brick won't sit flush
in these fine walls. Still, I lay it down.

This poem is from Richie McCaffery's book *Passport*. I like the seeming simplicity of it, how unostentatiously it builds[6] and how powerful is its understatement. And it has that truth about it that cannot be denied, about the Belgians and the *Radcliffe* brickworks:[7] all necessary for the poem to work.

The house Richie[8] grew up in was probably not dissimilar to my own semi-detached ancestral home,[9] although a few decades older. And the good bricks too, how they nurtured so many of us: cold, hard, regular, permanent and in their lifelessness life-sustaining. I'm with the people of Belgium when it comes to bricks.

Of course, I am projecting my own interests onto Richie's poem. It is, I suspect, far more about the relationship being cemented[10] by joint ownership than the nature of bricks as things. Perhaps. But I want poetry to say one thing and also mean another, and this poem does that. And it is a fine thing.

The poems that follow are not about bricks – my brick poems will come later – but about my mum, mostly after my dad died.[11] The first is a poem about the poem 'Won't', written by Walter de la Mare.[12] I've two poems in this book about other people's poems, as well as many poems by other people. It is confusing, I know.

My sister, Sylvia, is referenced in the second poem. Throughout her life my mum called us all by the name of whatever cat was in the house at the time. My mum grew up near Liverpool,[13] a city that at times was divided by religion. The instance described in the final poem made me laugh when it happened, and it still does.

---

6   Pun intended.
7   Although, frustratingly, it is not listed in my copy of *British Bricks* by David Kitching. It transpires it was actually one of many 'brands' produced by the Amble Brickworks in Northumberland.
8   We are acquainted so I think I can be so familiar.
9   The bottom end of Icknield Close, Didcot, Oxfordshire.
10 These puns won't stop just because you want them to.
11 August 2017.
12 I included this de la Mare poem in my book *On Poetry* and the cost of the permission to do so sadly forbids me doing so again. It can be found, of course, in de la Mare's own collections.
13 Formby, then Crosby.

Won't

Mum reads me 'Won't' by Walter de la Mare,
as she used to when we were first mother
and son. It's the same house, the same air,
the same words, but in her head another
woman holds her little boy. She tells me:
I read this to you when I was your mother.

Her voice distorts. She doesn't cry. A bee
taps at the window, twice, then drifts away.
But you're still reading it, I say, *and we
are still mother and son.*
                              *Oh. Will you stay
for your tea?* she asks, as she always does.
I won't, no; sorry. I have to get away.

Clouding Over

Clouding over, she forgets a face,
then a date, then the day of the week.
She calls her daughter the name of a cat
she had as a girl. The lightning striking
momentarily illuminates her life:
the night she woke to see the city burn;
that time they told her she was adopted.
The thunder reminds her of the bakery
she worked in. She remembers the *Falls*
at Llangollen, the river in full spate:
The rowing boat capsized, we all got wet.
The clouds are beautiful. It starts to rain.

Nineteen Fifty-Six

To lighten a dark day, Mum and I
are looking through an old album
of bits and pieces. We come across
a faded postcard of the vaulted,
ornately gilded and preposterous
interior of what Mum says was a
B&B (with evening meal extra)
favoured by the budget traveller
venturing abroad for the first time.

We look at the postcard. Outside
the garden shivers. *Mum*, I say, *this
is the Palace of Versailles, residence
of Louis the fourteenth.*
                              *Is it? Well,
I stayed there with Audrey, my oldest
friend. And she was a Catholic too.
We met at a dance in Liverpool.
I'll phone her later. Is she still alive?
I think she is. I'll phone her later.*

With reference to the poem 'Won't', a bee *did* tap at the window twice that day, then drifted away. And my mum did say the last line in the first stanza. I had asked her to read aloud to me Walter de la Mare's poem 'Won't', from his book *Poems*, as she had done often when I was a child. I must have been two or three when she bought this book. I still have it. The pages are brown with age and those that carry the poem 'Won't' have been repaired with Sellotape. The book has delicate line drawings by Margery Gill. 'Won't' is illustrated with a drawing of a mother cuddling her son on her lap.

I asked my mum, then eighty-six, to read the poem to see if she remembered it. Suddenly, half-way through, she did. It was a moment. And then she didn't. She is, my mum tells me, very forgetful these days. I wanted, in writing my poem, to echo the formality of de la Mare's poem. The rhyme scheme should go unnoticed but lodge in whatever part of the brain picks up these things. There is, in the penultimate line, a hanging-rhyme[14] on the word 'does'. It is hanging because I forgot about it. If you find a rhyme for 'does' later in the book then that's deliberate.[15]

But what about my dad? My dad: bloody hell. He could be a right so and so. Here are three poems in his memory.[16]

---

14   A term I have just now coined.
15   Yeah, right.
16   Roy Frederick Davidson, 1932–2017.

A Breakfast

Alone, really alone.
No one about to come down
or come in, and so I allow myself
some more of everything,
and I don't rush.

And then you are there,
with a small pan of porridge,
taking your packed lunch from the fridge,
listening to the quiet radio,
reading a library book,

before placing dishes in the sink
and taking your worker's leave,
without exchanging a glance,
perhaps not even aware
that I was ever born.

The Back Roads

And he would take the back roads
that often led to ploughed fields,
barbed wire, farmers with shotguns,
and once to a wooden footbridge,
over a river, with a sign saying
'Condemned': we crossed, of course.
That was my dad. Where is he now?

I swore I wouldn't take the back roads,
but here I am lifting my bike
over a stile, wading a ford,
crossing a rifle range; here I am
on the back roads; and that figure
ahead, vaulting a five bar gate
as one shouldn't, it is my father.

Father

I walked with my invisible father
out into the fields on the edge
of town. But they are gone now:
new roads, new names, new people.

Dad, stay here for a while, I said,
*and I'll go and find out what
has happened to our lives.* He sat
on the newly installed bench.

And when I returned, furnished
with stories of change, I found him
utterly dead, his cold eyes
on the cold world closed. So

many years he had lived here
and then this: his roads re-named,
his fields built over, his people
coming into view as strangers.

In August 2015 I spent a week in North Wales, staying in a partly renovated cottage at the end of a grassy track just off the A5 west of Llangollen. I went out cycling each day. There were good days and bad. Four days in, I was having a good day. I'd followed the River Dee, climbed north over the Horseshoe Pass, and then turned west along single track roads that rose, now and then, but mostly fell gently to the valley floor.

From the map I could see that the road took a dog-leg, adding a mile to the journey. A shortcut presented itself. I could take a bridleway and cut out the corners, so I did. The bridleway was wet and then flooded and then it was a brook and then a small stream and then – muddied and rueful – I was back on the tarmac road. I cycled on for a mile or so then leant the iron[17] against a field-gate, took my notebook[18] and pencil[19] from my saddle bag[20] and wrote, 'The Back Roads'. I had become my father's son.

Two years later, almost to the day, my dad died. I hadn't read him the poem, although I had mentioned my adventure.[21] He didn't seem very impressed but I think he appreciated the impulse. He would have done the same. All the incidents referenced in 'The Back Roads' are real, most of them a result of my dad's route-finding ability.

The last poem is simply a poem of private sadness, nothing more. It does, however, echo an incident in my dad's last years when he had taken a walk into one of Didcot's new housing estates and with his failing eyesight and poor sense of direction, and the sheer weariness of age, had found himself lost. Lost in his own town. Someone phoned the police and they brought him back home.

---

17   A Mercian, the frame fabricated from Reynolds 531 Double-Butted Competition steel tubing, since you ask. The frame of champions. Accept no substitute.
18   A Pukka Pad Jotta. The notebook of champions. Accept no substitute.
19   A Faber-Castell Jumbo Grip. The pencil of champions. Accept no substitute.
20   A Carradice Nelson Longflap. The saddle bag of champions. Accept no substitute.
21   I regret not reading him the poem.

Along with making poor directional choices, another of my dad's foibles was dragging things home that he was convinced would be of value to someone in the household. Dead rabbits, old radios, sofas, people. Now and then he got it right, but mostly he didn't. I was, at this point, going to include my friend Roz Goddard's poem about her dad collecting pianos, by way of reminding us that this is what dads sometimes do. It is a fine poem, from her book *Dismantling a Hotel Room* (Coal Press, 2006). But here's a new poem by Roz, which I think reflects better her current practice. It doesn't include dads but it does include a marl pit – my favourite type of pit[22] – which is nearly as good. And after that, the ubiquitous poem about quadratic equations that troubles every slim volume of contemporary poetry.

---

22   What is your favourite type of pit?

Winter, Lye Waste
By Roz Goddard

Snow came in thick as a flock of swans
in silence so deep we felt a prayer.
For weeks the dark music of ground
giving up nickel and iron was white breath.
We kneeled, called down the sun's halo:
its dogs, arcs, pillars of light. Only the depth
of earth and its voices rose to meet us in frozen
fields, would not stop until we became snow.

As the old year turned, we armed ourselves
at the trackless place with blanket-weed
and lime-wash to suffocate the voices,
lit fires around gooseberry, crab apple, marl pit.
Those who had swords drove them into ice,
as if we could hasten its surrender to water.
Finally, there was a low singing as dawn began
to break, crows drank sideways from snow melt.

A Quadratic Equation

A dad and a daughter are solving a quadratic equation.
They are seeking the value of x using the appropriate process,
beginning with factorisation. A solution is proving elusive;
they are outside the problem looking in at curtained windows.

Upstairs a son, who's employed in the building trade, plays guitar
unaware of the mathematical impossibility of 'equal temperament'.
And a mum is in the front room working out the likelihood
of character a killing character b before the end of the episode.

The daughter and the son cross on the stairs. She is fractious
and has been sent to bed, while the dad puts in a couple more hours,
but to no avail. Whatever the value of x they shan't know tonight.
And perhaps x has no value. Or perhaps it has many values.

Perhaps it is discovered in the dissonant chords that the son
untangles, or in the loaded silence between character a
and character b before the gun goes off, or perhaps it's simply
that which cannot be expressed although it is known to exist.

Note: Factorisation: a process that is used to break down numbers
into smaller numbers.

If you think I'm going to explain quadratic equations you've got another think coming.[23] There was a moment, a few years back, when I thought I understood them, but by the time I'd arranged for sets of commemorative stamps to be issued the understanding had gone. I am pleased with the son and daughter 'crossing' on the stairs. X marks the spot.

How Equal Temperament Ruined Harmony is a book by Ross W Duffin, who adds, in brackets: *and Why You Should Care.*[24] I care. I care about equal temperament because, as I understand it, the maths doesn't work but the music does.[25] It is the perfection of imperfection. It isn't right but then again it is.

Now, some poems about people I am not. And one by Zaffar Kunial about someone he *may* be. Notes about all the poems follow in the commentary.

---

23   A quadratic equation is one having the form $ax2 + bx + c = 0$, where x represents an unknown, and a, b, and c represent known numbers such that a is not equal to 0. So I am told.

24   Can whoever I have lent this book to please return it. Thank you.

25   Equal temperament is a system of tuning, in which the frequency interval between every pair of adjacent notes has the same ratio.

A Letter to Johann Joachim Quantz

Do not be sentimental or in your Art – W S Graham

Sir,

You tutored me to not expect applause,
and I was not disappointed. Though it was
still chilblain weather, my fingers lifted
like lapping water, letting and stopping
the sounds, to make – I hardly reckoned how –
one of your *capriccios*. So they stood me –
my hands hard from hauling ropes, my face
weather-reddened – in a sweating corner
of a silk room and pretended to listen.

What forced and servant music rippled
through the chambers of the recently rich
and along the canals! I was a carrier –
as the barge, the smack, the wherry is –
of freight or ballast, and out I went
into The Baltic or The German Sea.
So, they kept me for this purpose only,
and great service did I do them all,
bearing away the frightening silence.

Note: Johann Joachim Quantz (1697–1773) was a flautist, composer
and teacher, remembered mostly for his book *On Playing the Flute*.

William Smith's Poem

To show things in their state, how nature cuts
Its cloth, the flesh and bones, the sinews
And the tendons, muscle.

Know rocks and you'll know bricks and bread and beer,
What industry will grow and how it tastes;
Fortunes beneath our feet.

The colours are the accent of the land, the roll
Of language – languorous or clipped – is scarp
Or dip slope, hog's back, vale.

I've tapped a little hammer at the heart of *Him*
That we might show the substance of His glory,
And find coal, drain pastures.

Note: William Smith (1769–1839), was an English geologist, credited with creating the first nationwide geological map.

Collage, 1941

Lieber Kurt Schwitters, when you opened the door
to answer the knock and met the woman –
young enough to be *deine Tochter* – asking
if you wanted tea, did you fall in love
with her kindness or her artlessness? And how
did you get on in society, the two of you
being so different? Piecing together the bits
of your lives to form a collage – of course –
of memories and experiences, of textures
and relief, I suggest you arrived at an
unusual alike-ness which pleased you both,
which brings great sorrow even now, knowing
how, so soon after, you died, and the collage
disassembled into the usual differences.

Note: Kurt Schwitters (1887–1946), was a German artist working
in many genres and forms including Dada, Surrealism, poetry,
installations, sound and design.

A Last Letter to Ophelia Queiroz

In the voice of Fernando Pessoa

My darling girl, now you are dead to me,
I may tell you about the sun in the sky
And each shadow in its courtyard
And of the smell of sweat.

We have known each other for so long
But now I see you, alabaster still
And pale with want: a singular person
About whom I know little.

I hold your imaginary hand to my lips.
I bite your middle finger and draw-off,
From the warm bone, a small jewel.
Its cold fills my mouth.

Notes: Ophelia Queiroz (1900–1991) was the young woman who
had a relationship with the Portuguese poet Fernando Pessoa. Pessoa
(1883–1935) was noted for using heteronyms.

The Lyric Eye

By Zaffar Kunial

Methinks I see these things with parted eye
– William Shakespeare, A Midsummer Night's Dream

I've stood at your portrait at different times.
Scanned my own face, on and off, in the glass.
A cloud eclipsed. Vaguely before, or behind
you. Half cast, at a loss.
                  Even the gloss
back then, at school, left me looking this blank.
In the dark. Not on the same page as you.

But when I stand, here, almost in a blink
I can place my eyes – glazed over your stare;
let you lend me your ear, your famous cheek;
let the flare of your nostril stretch thin air;
even try on your earring, from five feet,
four centuries apart. I swear   by this lapse
the light on your mouth seems cast
                         half on mine
when I borrow the line between your lips.

The poem, 'Johann Joachim Quantz's Flute Lessons' by W S Graham, is a work of genius.[26] My poem isn't about Quantz but is in the voice of his imaginary protégé, the boat-boy Karl. It was originally meant as a homage to Graham, but it became a poem about how art may be carried by whatever craft is available, and how it finds itself commodified and subject to the tides of economics. I was pleased with the 'frightening silence' with its echo of 'freight' from earlier in the poem. The Baltic is my favourite sea.[27]

William Smith is another real person. Contrary, high-minded, a bit of a handful, extraordinarily far-sighted and determined. Although the William Smith poem was written for inclusion in an anthology,[28] I already had geological maps to hand. The names of the rocks and strata are interesting, of course, but the *colours* on these maps are simply gorgeous. William Smith used them to great effect on his original geological map.[29]

You may know the Kurt Schwitters of 'Collage, 1941' for his Dada-esque audio-artefact, *Ursonata*, which I trouble to have performed every few years by one of the few who can.[30] When he was released from internment on the Isle of Man in 1941, Schwitters made his way to London. He moved into an attic flat in Paddington and met Edith Thomas who became his partner for the last six years of his life.

Ophelia Queiroz was the woman who sparked what coy biographers would call a love interest in the poet Fernando Pessoa. Pessoa did not write this letter: I did.

---

26   I devote a chapter to it in my book *On Poetry*.

27   What is your favourite sea?

28   And was included in *Map: Poems After William Smith's Geological Map of 1815*, ed. Michael McKimm.

29   Which can be seen at the Royal Geological Society's apartments in London. There's an interactive version at www.strata-smith.com

30   Most recently, at the Birmingham Literature Festival in October 2018, with Tomomi Adachi as guest soloist and a scratch choir of citizens, under the baton of Stephen Meier, a man from Hannover (where Schwitters was also born) and Artistic Director of the Birmingham Contemporary Music Group.

His relationship with Ophelia was unclear and quite probably fraught (or frightening). He was, when he met her, posing as himself, which for him was a challenge.[31] He would have been happier as Hamlet or as one of his many heteronyms. She out-lived him, despite her first name.

And so to Zaffar Kunial's poem, 'The Lyric Eye'. My copy is heavily annotated because I wanted to understand how all the many parts fitted together. It is beautifully complex at first, then simple in its assertion, and then, thankfully, complex again. I've found it to be well worth re-reading.

The two poems that come now, one by Kit Wright and one by me, are both elegies for dead friends. And the final poem in this next section is by Jackie Kay. I'll say a few words about them all shortly.

---

31   Although he later used the words of Hamlet to declare his love for her.

Sonnet for Dick
By Kit Wright

My friend looked very beautiful propped on his pillows.
Gently downward tended his dreaming head,
His lean face washed as by underlight of willows
And everything right as rain except he was dead.
So brave in his dying, my friend both kind and clever,
And a useful Number Six who could whack it about.
I have described the man to whomsoever
The hell I've encountered, wandering in and out
Of gaps in the traffic and Hammersmith Irish boozers,
Crying, where and why did Dick Johnson go?
And none of the carloads and none of the boozer users,
Though full up with love and with camaraderie, know
More than us all-of-his-others, assembled to grieve
Dick who, brave as he lived things, took his leave.

Tony

i.m. AW

I'm reconciling a bank account, thinking of you.
A thousand little contracts keep me in the black.
I've found things in my garage I didn't know
were there. It's not that I needed or loved you
more than was necessary. Every transaction
in the world is linked to every other; more
than faith or hope, we are held by numbers.
You had years left, then how many months,
then the days, which went. The minutes: dust.
In the garage looking for something or other,
I find you in the charnel darkness, in the chaos
and disorder, the lost stuff. I am un-reconciled.

Darling
By Jackie Kay

You might forget the exact sound of her voice
or how her face looked when sleeping.
You might forget the sound of her quiet weeping
curled into the shape of a half moon,

when smaller than her self, she seemed already to be leaving
before she left, when the blossom was on the trees
and the sun was out, and all seemed good in the world.
I held her hand and sang a song from when I was a girl –

Heel y'ho boys, let her go boys –
and when I stopped singing she had slipped away,
already a slip of a girl again, skipping off,
her heart light, her face almost smiling.

And what I didn't know or couldn't say then
was that she hadn't really gone.
The dead don't go till you do, loved ones.
The dead are still here holding our hands.

Kit Wright was guest reader when I did an Arvon creative writing course in the late 1980s, tutored by Carol Ann Duffy and Liz Lochhead. But I only came across 'Sonnet for Dick' in his collected poems published in 2000.[32] It has the artifice I sometimes want from poetry, precisely engineered and polished. The voice is knowing but vulnerable. It goes in hard and then takes off into the distance. It is more powerful for trying to be proper and upright. It is about what grief is like, in my limited experience.

When I wrote the poem 'Tony', about my late friend Tony Whitehead, I had Kit's poem in mind. Tony died too young. After the funeral service, I wandered through the carpark at the crematorium in Cardiff and I was suddenly overcome with grief. I had never cried so uncontrollably before. Perhaps because this was the first time I had felt grief, when I came to write about it I found I needed to contain my feelings in things that were dull and dutiful. A bank reconciliation[33] and tidying a garage would do, activities we use to distract ourselves. This poem was first published in my book *Early Train*, but as not nearly enough people have read it, here it is again.

And I follow my poem with Jackie Kay's, 'Darling'. I also included it in my book *On Poetry* because there is no law against it, having sought appropriate permission. It is a poem that never fails to stop me in my tracks. While my poem is all about distracting myself from grief, Jackie's[34] poem holds grief in its arms and sings it to sleep.

---

32   Oddly enough the title poem of Kit's most recent collection is 'Ode to Didcot Power Station' (Bloodaxe Books, 2014), which initially made Didcotians proud. Subsequently, the first-stage decommissioning of the Power Station's cooling towers in 2017 killed four demolition workers. Our pride turned to sorrow. The second-stage demolition two years later managed to cut the electricity to tens of thousands of homes, including my mum's house. It would be no exaggeration to say that Didcot Power Station did not want to be demolished.

33   Really? What never? But how do you know the state of your finances at any one time? How do you manage your grief?

34   We are friends, so I may be so bold.

I think I was ten years old when my dad put his head round my bedroom door one evening, just as I had gone to bed, and said that I wouldn't be seeing my grandad again. It was a very gentle way of telling me his father had died.

I don't remember feeling any great sorrow, although I liked my grandad very much. At fourteen, during World War One, he had run away to sea and served in the Merchant Navy. In the Second World War he drove trams through the blitz in Liverpool. His children, including my dad, were evacuated to North Wales.[35] My grandad was a member of the Communist Party of Great Britain, which gave him a certain stability. The poem is for Rita Walker, his daughter, my aunt, my dad's sister.

It is followed by a rather angry poem and then a fearful poem and then the poems about bricks I've been promising you. Then there's a belter of a poem by Mick North called 'Land', and my echoing of that poem in one of my own, called 'Cycling'.

---

35   To a place called Llansannan, not far from where I stopped to write 'The Back Roads'. My dad remembered, while he was there, seeing the distant glow of his home city burning. He was eight.

Frederick Arthur Davidson

For Rita Walker

I think of my Merchant Navy grandfather
boarding a vessel bound for the far north,
even to the end a neat and abstemious man,
perfectly turned out, a dab-hand at sewing.
He served me baked beans with curry powder
like they did at sea. He wanted revolution.

That he was, on balance, wrong about how
the world would sail itself is, on balance,
irrelevant. He stood still on one of the decks
as the ship cut its way through a choppy swell
and he moved with the mass of steel and water;
a man at ease with the mass of steel and water.

Utopia

It's an old brick in an old wall along the Old
Main Line Canal a kilometre west of here and I
Take a photo of it, and post the photo, and tweet
The photo and say something suitably ironic
About bricks and walls. I might as well have thrown
Myself in, there and then, because I had betrayed
My people with cheap words and fancy language
And knowing looks and an educated tongue: like:
What I don't know about life isn't worth knowing;
Like: *I know so much about what we want and what
They wanted;* like: *I've done so much to get it.*
Like fuck I have. And now they talk like the Right
Have won and that's not a fucking problem. It is
A fucking problem. This brick stuck in this wall
With its arse showing the clay-cast word *Utopia*
Is the fucking problem. And you lot reading this
Are the fucking problem. The leaves are turning
Early this year and we failed to pick all of the
Beautiful blackberries because we were watching
A long-form drama about some world that doesn't
Exist but would be fun if it did. And I am sorry
But I can't be happy about any of this until
The word *Utopia* and the brickworks that cast it –
That bloody word on the base of a brick – is making
Bricks to build the houses for the people who need
Houses, and giving food to the hungry and clothing
To the cold, and for everyone the sweet dark taste
Of the blackberries you pick even when the dusk
Is nearly upon you, and you are tired and alone.
Those blackberries and that taste. That *Utopia*.

Borders

They are bringing back the borders.
So a night train whines to a dead halt
and in the blazing darkness of suspicion
uniformed men – just doing a job – thump
through doors and fill the corridors
with their orders and mistrust.

They are looking for the others, not you.
But still, your eyes look to your shoes
in need of spit and polish. You hope
they do not stop. They stop.
You hear the hum of electricity.
Voices demand papers. And it begins.

Brick-Life

Cut from the clay of the big pit, blade-bitten,
thumped and smacked, stacked up, left for dead;

a comfort after a winter of frost, to be made
at last, lying in wait, waiting for the moment.

The kiln won't kill you, they tell us, *you're all
in it together, line-up, lie back, count to ten.*

We wake in a kind of Hades, our hearts hard,
hollow-seeming, and we hold our brittle breath.

We cool on the racks, regretful, rueful, tired;
the best of us are silent, the rest confused.

They call us brother brick and sister brick,
they come for us and find us uniform, a unit.

We cross a continent of country, our song
is *build we, build we, build we now the new.*

We make the world, we do what we are told,
go where they place us, in whatever bond,

and build the walls, hold the earth at bay,
culvert the rivers, shoulder the high roads,

tell ourselves we are happy, shout hurrah,
try to move but can't; try to think, can't.

Brickwork

They use a Flemish Bond but set in it
Sufficient blue-flared headers
To make the lozenges
Of language for an eye
To read with ease a hundred years ahead.

A brick arch frames a window for the light
To be let in, and for a door,
A lintel. All are laid
Like script declaimed on Sundays
At faces plain as chimneys on a roof.

The building of a cottage, house or grange,
That finds its height and stands
Against the day, is song.
For hands that speak in courses,
That harden as they weary of the work.

And they are dumb or gone away or dead
Who cut the sweet, pale clay
Of sentences and fired them
In common kilns to make
The narratives that keep us home and dry.

What we read now when walking through a place
Is all that's left of those
Who squared the quiet day
With chisel, hawk and bolster,
Who held their tongues but spoke vernacular.

Notes: Flemish Bond is one of many patterns in which bricks can be laid, varying the header (short side) and stretcher (long side) for strength and to please the eye. Blue-flared headers are dark blue bricks laid with their short sides outward facing. The colouring comes from being placed close to the heat source in a kiln. Hawk is a square plate on a stick to hold mortar ready to be trowelled onto bricks. A bolster is a heavy-duty chisel used to cut bricks clean in half.

Land

by Mick North

Who loosed the wind
in the singing fence-wire
in the fence dividing the hill?

Who tends the rowan
in the fern-decked gill?

They will answer you
with the strength of the Pound
and the unfair advantage of high ground.

Who sells the berries
the fieldfares feast on,
migrant Viking winter thrushes?

Who dug the gill
where the ringing beck rushes?

They will answer you
with the Law's petrified truth,
with broken promises and written proof.

Who built the mill
where they weave the weather,
spin the jubilant roaring waters?

Who sets the sleet
and the snowfall quotas?

They will answer you
with the permission of history
and the dead wood of pedigree.

Who taught the fox
to prowl the rusty bracken
where dusk draws fire from his pelt?

Who gave the leather
for the tackle, boots and belt?

They will answer you
with unbridled market forces
and a fine tradition of breeding horses.

Who saw the falcon
stoop on the grouse,
a sickle blade cut from the sun?

Who decodes the signal
from the sportsman's flashing gun?

Do not listen to their answers.
Do not accept their judgement of a sod's worth.
Do not let the wicked inherit the earth.

Cycling
For Mick North

I.

Who owns the sturdily built houses
taunting my relative poverty
along undulating lanes?

The drives are gated, and bolted
are the shutters at the *Mill House*
and the *Hill Top Grange.*

And the hedges are rich with flowers,
and many species of bird confuse
the security cameras.

II.

I am trying to pedal fluidly,
to use my scant resources efficiently,
to save my strength for climbing

the stout, short ridges rising
like natural fortifications, getting
the cyclist out of the saddle.

More fool me for acquiescing,
for contenting myself with a spin
on a Sunday morning on byways

open to the public, not straying
from the straight and narrow, admiring
the tax-efficient estates.

III.

But, in time, the owners of these
period properties will be required
to declare themselves, and not

by swinging from a fresh gallows
at a crossroads on the border
of two rural counties,

but by coming with full hands and *laying*
at the feet of the people all
the wealth they are not due.

That poem by Mick North is quietly magnificent. It was probably written forty years ago. It carries the echoes of other poems and poets, which is as it should be. And it is not afraid to rouse our passions. Its anger is barely concealed. It was perhaps the same anger that prompted me to write 'Utopia'. And fear and anger caused me to write 'Borders'. And the poem 'Cycling' is bitter and angry. I'm nothing but rage these days; a danger to myself.

Let me pause for a moment and tell you how much I like bricks. I like the language and lore of brickmaking and bricklaying. I like terms like *Flemish Bond* and *Stretcher Bond* and *diapering*,[36] and I happen to know what a *bolster* is and what a *hawk* is, and how to tell a *hawk* from a *handsaw*.[37] And although this is partly why bricks feature in some of my poems, they are also there simply to build arguments, to discover and advance opinions. Something else poetry is good for.

Utopia was the name stamped into a brick I chanced upon at a time when I was feeling particularly unhappy about our times. Like Richie McCaffery's *Radcliffe* brick, it was just a brand name. As it happens it was being used second-hand, and the retaining wall it was part of was a rough and ready affair. Certainly not the work of a craftsperson. This was not the Utopia we had been promised.

And here follows a poem for my daughter, Mollie. My son, Frederick, has had poems for or about him in the past; now it is Mollie's turn.

---

36   Bricks of a different colour, placed in a wall to make simple patterns – diamonds, lozenges, etc. You can learn more from *Brick Building in Britain*, by R W Brunskill.
37   *Hamlet*, Act II, Scene II. Other interpretations exist but mine is correct. Shakespeare was a Midlander. The Midlands is mostly brick country.

A Music Box

For Mollie Davidson

Bought in Vilnius for five euros,
a throwaway thing, its music almost
lost, a small constellation
of sounds. The handle is fun to turn,
as the five boats pictured on its sides
rise towards us, blind with certainty.

Don't look inside. We know a pretty
mechanism for making music chimes out
these steely notes, but let the boats
be tugged by their stiff sails to what
far shore should then appear, and let
the music take you whereso'er it will.

'A Music Box' is a study of animated still life. How much could I find from the purchase and gift of a cheap music box? Music boxes mean childhood to me. And here I am giving one to my daughter – now grown-up – and using it to speculate on her future, to almost propel her away from the shore into open waters. The use of *whereso'er* is my contribution to bringing a perfectly good word back into common parlance.

Now, another poem about music, or more accurately, about the silence that surrounds music (and surrounds poetry, too). And then, one about the curiosity of listening to music and the intimacy of distance. And then to printing. Just printing. What printing might mean. And then to Pauline Stainer's poem, 'The Honeycomb'.

The Silence

In response to Cantus in Memoriam Benjamin Britten
by Arvo Pärt

I like best the silence that is not
Silence but our breathing, the orchestra
Of flesh and thought caught in looped
Arpeggios. But back to the silence,
That comes at the start and finish
And places a hand on our shoulder
Or takes our hands and leads us not
To heaven or hell but into the ever-
Lasting place of unknowing, from where
We struggled out. But back to the silence,
That for us on the surface of the earth
Is nothing like silence, but a continuous
Roar of obligation and dispatch, of coming
And going, and for Benjamin Britten
Was the great bell tolling and then not
Tolling. And that is what I like best;
The silence that is noisy like the bell,
That we go back to, where we came from.

Notes: Arvo Pärt (born 1935) is an Estonian composer. His work
is minimalist in style and is influenced by Gregorian chant. He left
Estonia during the Soviet period.

Live Broadcast

Too late to go out and nowhere to go
anyway, I content myself with this
celestial but dis-concerting music,

a *Brandenburg* by J S Bach, which they enjoy
in London very much. Your message says
you're sitting down to listen to it too,

or busying yourself with things that must
be done, or watching as the last high clouds
grow dark. Although we are alone the gods

of digital transmission have ensured
the sound they give to me they give to you.
Now all that is between us is the music,

which is not anything at all, but keeps
our little minutes and our little thoughts
in its design, so that we can be known

each to the other, keeping time, until
the final notes have died away and grand
applause releases us back to our selves.

Printing

As sheet after sheet of lightly embossed
lust is lifted from the press of ourselves,
this industry we've purposely established
is not unlike the printing of a book.

The little letters forming on our tongues
are consonants and vowels of what's un-said
but finds itself repeatedly imprinted
in sweat for touch to read a meaning there.

We speak the sentences that make the moment
as close to permanent as flesh can stand,
and take the words to heart and let them lie,
enfolded, trimmed and bound. But books are dead

before the ink is dry: take off your glasses,
put down what you are reading, let us apply
our typesetters' eyes and nimble fingers
to make another page of hard-pressed text.

The Honeycomb

By Pauline Stainer

They had made love early in the high bed,
Not knowing the honeycomb stretched
Between lath and plaster of the outer wall.

For a century
The bees had wintered there,
Prisoning sugar in the virgin wax.

At times of transition,
Spring and autumn,
Their vibration swelled the room.

Laying his hand against the plaster
In the May sunrise,
He felt the faint frequency of their arousal,

Nor winters later, burning the beeswax candle,
Could he forget his tremulous first loving
Into the humming dawn.

When I write poetry I think of myself disturbing the silence with some little sounds. That first poem, 'The Silence', came easily once I had formed my argument. If I had not been writing about a piece by Arvo Pärt I probably wouldn't have used such a register of language. Somehow the music gave me permission to write beyond my self-deprecating self.

'Live Broadcast' and 'Printing' are obviously poems about the live broadcast of a concert and about Guttenberg's invention of the printing press. In both cases I have tried to find an *otherness* in what may be simply known, because I hoped there would be some truth hidden there. In 'Live Broadcast' I have used an idea of shared listening similar to that used by Philip Larkin in his poem 'Broadcast' (from *The Whitsun Weddings*). And at one stage the poem contained the phrase 'some stuff' which echoes Larkin's line in 'Church Going' ('... some brass and stuff / Up at the holy end'). Larkin's choice of the word 'stuff' was so exact and perfect and having read his poetry this meant it had to go from my poem. Our sharing an idea about concerts on the radio, well, I can live with that and thank him for it.

Pauline Stainer's[38] poem, as with so many of the poems I am sharing by others, is simplicity itself. It is very musical, meaning I hear the interplay of sounds, with a metre and perhaps even a musical key, and the whole poem bookended by the reference to 'early' and 'later'. I can only imagine that the ordinariness of the honeycomb suggested the otherness of the experience of the lovers. It reads like a poem that sprang into existence without any intent upon the reader.

By contrast, my poem about Bertolt Brecht and Margarete Steffin playing chess is full of intent upon the reader. It follows here, preceded by a longer piece that purports to be about apple picking in the 1980s, and it is. If you read this poem closely you can just discern the ghost of a last line, long since removed but still working. And between the two poems, the late Helen Dunmore's exquisite poem, 'Wild Strawberries'.

---

38   We have not met, so some formality is required.

Apple Picking

It's autumn and I'm working
at picking the last of the small apples.

They've grown without check. They glitter
in the slight breeze. It takes a young man

and a tapered ladder and some nerve
to reach them. In the big, wooden shed

the women of the village and one
old man are grading my catch.

I'm the last picker, sent to finish off
because I'm recently fallen in love

and am incapable of doing much else
other than swaying in treetops.

So now I'm nudging the ladder
into the branches and taking two

rungs at a time, holding a basket.
I lever, pivot, lean and stretch-out

to twist the apples from their sprues.
I listen for the soft, short snap of stem

parting company. What I pick I set down
as gently as I can: apples bruise

beneath the skin, unnoticed until
days later they bloom into decay;

and damaged apples are discarded;
the women of the village see to that.

Working, I think of the young woman
I've fallen in love with, how we found

the pale scars on her body when we
undressed each other – an accident

as a child; scalding water, nothing more.
I had put my face to her damaged skin,

and drawn in her rain-washed smell,
not realising how this must have hurt,

or how much love it took to let me
see her. And I did not wish that she

was different, I wished that I was.

Wild Strawberries

By Helen Dunmore

What I get I bring home to you:
a dark handful, sweet-edged,
dissolving in one mouthful.

I bother to bring them for you
Though they're so quickly over,
pulpless, sliding to juice,

a grainy rub on the tongue
and the taste's gone. If you remember
we were in the woods at wild strawberry time

and I was making a basket of dockleaves
to hold what you'd picked,
but the cold leaves unplaited themselves

and slid apart, and again unplaited themselves
until I gave up and ate wild strawberries
out of your hand for sweetness.

I lipped at your palm –
the little salt edge there,
the tang of money you'd handled.

As we stayed in the wood, hidden,
we heard the sound system below us
calling the winners at Chepstow,
faint as the breeze turned.

The sun came out on us, the shade blotches
went hazel: we heard names
bubble like stock-doves over the woods

as jockeys in stained silks gentled
those sweat-dark, shuddering horses
down to the walk.

Brecht, B. v Steffin, M., Marlebäck, 1940

In Finland, perched on the pitched roof
of Europe, they've set-up a chess set
under the leaves of late summer larches.
He leans towards the board, as she brings
a knight into play, pinning a rook.
Though he is a fighter, a scourge
of the bourgeoisie, an enemy of fat-
cats and industrialists, of princes
and bishops, he wants her to win,
to have the shirt off his back,
to bring him to his knees.

Later he'll know the shadows were already
on her lungs, and she'll have made the long
journey around the northern lakes –
wearing the great-coat he *liberated*,
knowing how cold the winters were –
to a sanatorium in Moscow,
to release her last breath. But now,
while she is here, he wants her so much
to turn the board and all its pieces
into hail and thunder, and to rest
his heavy head against her neck.

Notes: There exists a photograph of Bertolt Brecht playing chess with
Margarete Steffin. She was a literary collaborator and for a time they
were lovers.

Brecht and Steffin used poems to communicate their love for each other.[39] In the Estonian's writer Mati Unt's novel *Brecht at Night*, there is a very good portrait of him at exactly the time he and Steffin were photographed playing chess. Frustratingly, while being full of compelling detail about Brecht, the novel doesn't mention the chess.[40]

The previous poem by Helen Dunmore contains many excellent things. It appears to be almost incidental in its progress, guileless, not needing to bring attention to itself. You'll know by now that I like this a lot in poetry, that it should not have palpable designs upon us (as Keats said).

When I was in my late teens I worked in an orchard and poems about this have cropped up in all my books. It was hard work but a potent experience. The orchard was owned by Miss Balcombe. Her personal history, how she came to be living alone in a wooden summerhouse set in her own orchard, was the subject of much speculation. The poem coming up, from my book *The Living Room,* offers more about her.

After the apple-picking I got a job working for The Institute. Which Institute I am not at liberty to say, but those who worked there were interested in both geology and water. My job was to pay the wages of the weekly-paid staff, including Claud. He was a nice bloke but the Greenham Common Women's Peace Camp[41] was to him a mystery.

If I had read Ernesto Cardenal at that time – and the Nicaraguan Revolution was still a live issue – I might have shared the poem 'Zero Hour' with Claud, to help him with the bigger picture.[42] I came across it later, after I had come across Cardenal.[43] The final lines are prophetic.[44]

And I finish this section with another poem in response to a poem.

---

39   This relationship is made clear in the poems they wrote to each other, a collection of which was edited by David Constantine and Tom Kuhn.
40   A search of the internet will bring up a photograph of them mid-game. And search further and there are some interesting photographs of Brecht playing chess with Walter Benjamin.
41   1981–2000, set up to protest about American Cruise Missiles stationed in the UK.
42   No, I would never have done that.
43   He was at a poetry festival I attended a few years ago.
44   The watchman said, "The morning comes, and also the night." (Isaiah 21:11–12).

Miss Balcombe's Orchard

I came from the shed where we sorted the apples
not splitting the day
but moving through it.

And I carried a spade and a fork or a hoe.

She was gone down to the top orchard,
all her seventy years,
on the diddy tractor,
with the dog snapping at grasses.

A vapour of petrol settled on the morning.

Slicing the friable soil
the spade made the sound of steel on flint
and the frozen loam fractured,
sheared at my feet
and at my weight.

And I was delving as I had been instructed.

Only I did not know she was dead then,
propped on the tractor,
her leather gauntlets gripping
the knurled steering wheel,
the motor idling.

And her mouth was open to release
the ghost of the spark
of steel on flint
that had moved through her.

And her unfashionable trees were a lost garden.

Claud, 1982

Of the village, but working for the Institute,
Loading, driving, fetching, carrying.

A sure grasp of his place, it seemed then.
Now I'm not so sure. His son went off

To strong-arm the Greenham Common Women,
For Claud that was the world gone mad.

I sorted his wages for two and a half years.
You knew where you were with hard cash.

Zero Hour

By Ernesto Cardenal, translated by Robert Pring-Mill

Central America: tropical nights,
volcanoes and lagoons beneath the moon
and lights in presidential palaces;
barracks, and sad bugle-calls at dusk.
"I frequently decide the death of man
while smoking a cigarette"
says Ubico, smoking a cigarette ...
In his palace, which is like a pink-iced cake,
Ubico has a cold. The crowd outside
has been dispersed with tear-gas bombs.
San Salvador, at night: distrust and spying,
muttering in the homes and small hotels,
and screams in police stations.
The crowd stoned the palace of Carías,
breaking just one window of his office,
but the police opened fire on the crowd.
And Managua: covered by deployed machine-guns
from its palace, which is like a chocolate cake:
steel helmets out patrolling in the streets.

> *Watchman, what of the night?*
> *Watchman, what of the night?*

Notes: Ernesto Cardenal (born 1925) is a Nicaraguan former
Catholic priest, poet and politician. He was a member of the
Sandinista Party during the Nicaraguan revolution and was
Nicaragua's Minister of Culture for eight years. Ubico was the
Guatemalan dictator overthrown in the Guatemalan Revolution of
October 1944.

On 'Why Brownlee Left'

I was nineteen and not well read,
other than John Keats and most
of Spenser and a bit of Lawrence
and Hardy, the usual boy's stuff.

This was different. What it said
it said simply enough, neat turns
at each line's end then back again,
ploughing a straight, narrow furrow

until, at the finish it just came
to a halt. And stood there. No joy,
no sorrow, the cut earth offering
nothing but emptiness, inside me.

If you know Paul Muldoon's poem, 'Why Brownlee Left', you'll see how it influenced my poem about Miss Balcombe, if only in the absence it alerts us to. It took twenty-five years for me to realise the debt I owed to Muldoon's poem and I felt the realisation deserved a poem in its own right. That stuff about what I had read is true. In those days I thought that as a young person interested in poetry I should have a few thousand pages of good reading under my belt before taking up arms. Mind you, finding and certainly owning poetry books wasn't easy. No one was selling the complete works of Spenser in my town.

I saw Paul Muldoon read with, I think it was, Maureen Duffy, at The Old Fire Station in Oxford in 1983 and I'm sorry to say I thought it was very dull. Either I had not learned to appreciate their genius or it was, indeed, very dull. I spotted Muldoon's poem 'Why Brownlee Left' in a listings magazine by way of advertising the reading and it worked directly. Through print it released itself in a way it hadn't in performance.

I read a lot of Paul Muldoon's poetry in the 1980s and 1990s, but I was not enough aware of the politics of the time and how it shaped his writing. I somehow thought, that poets were beyond politics. Even though I grew up in the most political of families, I did not see myself as marked by the political.

In a parallel tradition to Muldoon is Catherine Byron, a generous poet who guided my reading and writing in my early twenties. Her poem, 'Night Flight to Belfast', feels strangely connected to Ernesto Cardenal's.

The three poems that follow Catherine's were written in response to a crash-course in the history of twentieth century Ukrainian writing which I received during a visit to Kyiv. I wanted to produce the simplest of records of that experience, to let the facts of the place speak for themselves.

Night Flight to Belfast

By Catherine Byron

This night I visited my childhood home
and walked through rooms and passages and doors
my memory could not trace:
a room with orange silk upon the walls
and orange beds; a cubbyhole with pens
and drawings on a table, half complete;
an open book of flowers, Redouté prints.
My feet wheeled unsurprised past further doors
to where the hallway like a ballroom waited:
the staircases were double, each fleeing its mate
in twin wide curves to an upstairs dark that I
would not ascend to.

The house warmth failed, the dusk had lapped
up unfamiliar linoed corridors.
Outside, the crackling tramp of a patrol
and 'Number sixteen! Open up!' the soldiers cried.
But our house was number four. And then
the image overlay of single stairs,
of woodwork's brown combed grain on heavy doors
and plain poor white distemper on the walls.

> I was trapped in the wrong house
> the wrong dream
> and soldiers kept on banging
> at the unknown door.

Striletska Street 15

Avant-garde writers of the nineteen twenties,
Repressed in the nineteen thirties, I imagine
Your gatherings on summer evenings in Kyiv,
How you re-constructed the old world,

What form it might take, its new shape,
And how it would be spoken about,
Pushing the revolution along already
Rusting tracks towards Siberia.

Notes: Striletska Street 15 is the address in Kyiv of the Ukranian writer Borys Antonenko-Davydovych. He was a member of Lanka, one of the most influential literary groups in 1920s Ukraine. It was also briefly the home of Lesia Ukrainka, writer and activist, who championed Ukrainian national liberation and feminism.

Kyiv Writers

I'm impressed by famous writers' houses,
and our guide's knowledge of when each
arrived and departed – sometimes under
armed-guard, sometimes shot while trying
to slip away, rarely in their beds.
I slip away, as quickly as I can,
unnoticed, drawing no attention,
and find myself at the station watching
trains present the narrative going forward.
From Minsk, from Odessa, from Moscow,
stepping down from one expectant life
into another, with the cruel optimism
of art sewn into coats and backpacks,
writers editing themselves into the city.

Metro

Weeks later, I think about Kyiv. I assume
It is still there, still opaque with people,
The same cafés, the same monuments,
The blocks of flats for workers, elderly
Lorries bringing things from somewhere.
It must still take five minutes by escalator
To reach the platforms. The roar of trains
Approaching is the turbulence of centuries.

Notes: The Arsenalna Metro station in Kyiv is the deepest underground station in the world at 105.5m. Its entrance is from the bank high up above the Dnieper River.

Catherine's poem has such detail – reminiscent of Louis MacNeice[45] – and pitches itself perfectly from within the memory of a child. And at the door, as so often, are the soldiers.[46] As they were in Kyiv. As they were in Nicaragua. As they still are in so many places. We who haven't experienced what Catherine writes about don't know we're born. And we don't know our history.

And on that subject, here are three short poems about the English Civil War and the English Revolution that followed. That revolution was full of imperfections but some came of it. It threw a good number of ideas onto the fire, and while they didn't triumph (ideas never do) the ashes fertilised the future. And don't tell me the Restoration turned everything back. It didn't.

The first poem uses the same technique I used in my short 2014 collection, *Humfrey Coningsby: poems, complaints, explanations and demands for satisfaction*, which is to place the historical and the contemporary side by side and damn the consequences. Partly this is to remove myself from the poem by placing it beyond my experience. But then, my dad used to work in that car factory mentioned, and he would have been a Leveller and my mum might have been inclined to be a Digger. So it is a very personal poem, which was obvious all along.

And not personal at all, but sustaining one of the themes of the Civil War poems, is 'Without Venice'. I have nothing against Venice but we are all apt to forgive oppressors of many colours and across the ages if they happen to have left some pretty paintings or a palace or two for our delight. We shouldn't forgive, although we should delight in a good painting or bit of architecture or – best of all – a recorder concerto.

---

45   As a child, Catherine lived opposite the 'big house' that had been the official residence of Louis MacNeice's father, a Protestant clergyman.

46   Although they tend not to knock, or not for long.

We Set Our Guns
England 1642/2019

We set our guns up on the London Road,
Hard by the car factory, with a view
Of smoke from within the city walls
And waited. Seeing a small party of horse,
Their muskets gleaming in the winter sun,
Their plumes rising as they rode, an
Affront to Heaven, we prepared ourselves.

In light they came, we took them cleanly.
Every man down, a bullet in his neck
And the horses liberated. It was that
Easy, nothing much of a battle, skirmish
Really, but we were happy for it, thanked
God, our weapons and our nerves. Went off
To see what other work there was to do.

The Lack of a Dandy Tyrant

In open court we caught and killed the King.
All Europe stopped. The waves were stilled
On the shores, the clouds scudded no more
Through national skies. Aye, that is what
They wrote later, as I recollect. Still,
The herd plodded over the sea-green mead
And a ploughboy made certain the blade
Cut clean on the sod and a girl churned
The milk to butter and England was, at
That moment, no worse for the sudden lack
Of a dandy tyrant.

On the Arrest of Thomas Prince, 1649

They led us on, we led them on, we fought
And made petitions, published pamphlets,
Preached and proselytised and met in inns
And received word and had word sent, talked
And talked. But that morning, the stink
From the river crept up on me and spoke.
Two hundred soldiers they deployed, one
With a warrant would have been enough,
But in England not only must injustice
Be done but it must be seen to be done.

Notes: Thomas Prince: (1615–1653?) cheesemonger, soldier, Leveller and publisher of pamphlets critical of Oliver Cromwell and his government. In March 1649 he was arrested at his printing shop in the parish of St Martin Ongar in London by a detachment of 200 troops. He quipped at the time that one man with a warrant would have been enough.

Without Venice

Looking out across the grey lagoon to the super-state of Venice,
I am struck by how easily it could all disappear, the centuries'
bruises blooming without witness beneath the wrestling waters.

Would civilisation have been much reduced if this city – its sly,
truculent investors, with ships and weigh-bills and propensity
for securing mercenaries at reasonable rates – had not flourished?

What stones would not have been dressed? What pigments un-ground?
And shoals of notes un-heard. No bloody opera! We'd have plodded on,
whistling, making bricks, laughing at each other falling over.

I have been wanting to share the poem 'Six Filled the Woodshed with Soft Cries' by my friend Maura Dooley for many years. It does not do us the disservice of explaining itself, but it makes absolute sense. And although it is a poem that draws its imagery from what might be called the natural world, it surely isn't a nature poem.

Following are some other nature poems that aren't about nature, including 'The Greenwood' which is about me and trees. I could never stomach the idea that our salvation was in immersing ourselves in the natural world, but I'll allow that being in woods is sometimes interesting. While English woods are, with a few exceptions, hardly ancient, the *idea* of woods certainly is.

To show how a real nature poem might be written, a poem that simply soaks itself in the physicality, the sensuality, of nature, I finish this section by offering 'Padley Woods: June 2007' by the late Ann Atkinson. She was a very good poet and not read nearly enough in her lifetime. Spending time with her *Collected Poems* is as good as a walk through any woods, rain or shine.

Six Filled the Woodshed with Soft Cries
by Maura Dooley

From grass-stained eggs we bred eight;
two hens, six fine white cockerels,
they scrambled, fluffing feathers
for a summer and an autumn month.

Now, hands pinked by the wind,
I watch their maned necks nervously.
Yesterday the tiniest learnt to crow,
latched a strange voice to crisp air,
his blood red comb fluting the wind,
feathers creaming, frothing at his throat.

One month till Christmas, the clouds thicken,
he turns on me an icy, swivel eye,
Do you dare deny me?

My neighbour helps me chase them,
snorting snuff, which rests on his sleeve
in a fine white scatter. A wicker basket
gapes wide as he dives for them.

Six filled the woodshed with soft cries.
Their feathers cover stony ground
like a lick of frost.

Leaving

When we left it was the end of everything.
We didn't even bother to lock up.
We walked to the craft –
those who could –
and counted ourselves in.

It's the children I feel sorry for;
what they won't know about rain showers and thunder;
what they won't know about crossing a cold brook barefoot
or lying in a hanger of beech trees at evening
and hearing the leaves talking.

I know I romanticise.
I know nothing is immutable.
I know it shouldn't trouble me
that a beautiful future awaits us:

my children, and their children,
their bodies powered-down to drift
down icy streams to pleasant distant worlds,
their eyes closed, their mouths still.

The Ridgeway, 2117

A tensed tendon of chalk across the shire,
Good for gallops and beech hangers.

It hardly registers from outer space,
So we zoom in our screens and set ourselves

To canter around our quarters for an hour
In honour of imaginary horses, until

The sweat flecks from our rough muzzles
And we stink of earth and open air.

Note: The Ridgeway is a prehistoric track, considered to be Britain's oldest road, extending from Wiltshire along the chalk ridge of the Berkshire Downs to the River Thames at Goring.

Like Lichen

For Sylvia Davidson

My sister sends me photographs of lichen
because it's interesting. And we chat about
our late dad's politics and if he was ever
instructed by the Party how to vote
and which facilities to cycle to
directly in event of revolution,
which would be soon, was in the air like spoors,
the multiplying matter of Utopia,
two things as one, the people and belief.

And when it came, the colours would rejoice:
the milky greys, the acid oranges,
the greens and browns. And all our lives
would have the delicate, the sculptured grace
of lichen filigree, with shapes like tongues
or hands; such intricate, responsible
self-love, such sacrifice, such service to
the twisted trees of each of us. Like lichen,
the whole and patient edifice was hope.

The Greenwood

A nice idea, but no one is going to take to it
to escape the law, and what it offers isn't
a country of itself, complete with courts and fools.

There may be barbed wire and tracks made by
heavy plant hauling timber down to yards. There may
be sign-posted rights of way for all abilities.

The Greenwood isn't what it used to be. But stand me
in a still, cold-folded clearing and I will see shades
of the old world, the commonwealth of trees.

Padley Woods: June 2007

by Ann Atkinson

How the trees love this weather:
slaked hydraulics pulse on full power,
their trunks, drenched conduits as they lean
into the long moment of their fall.

Water streams the paths, finds new ways
down and lays washed sand in its wake.
Tree roots, spreading like knuckled veins
over the slopes, are terraces of sand and silt.

The music of the gorge is white water,
its constant industry of flow, the brook
full of itself and urgent for the river,
shifting wood, moving rock, carving stone.

At the bridge the water's hurl is leather brown
and heady – on the road, springs erupt and well
through tarmac, streams find their way easy
through dry-stone walls. The canopy is listening,

its tesserae of leaves held out palm-up
and tapping a morse of *rain, more rain* – then louder,
loud as the brook's full-throated song, clattering –
rain, here it is, again and more of it, rain more rain.

I find myself in the poems 'Leaving' and 'Ridgeway: 2117' looking forward in order to look back. The Ridgeway is my favourite prehistoric road,[47] and boldest where it passes along the ridge of chalk that shoves up into North Berkshire and South Oxfordshire.[48] My sister and I scattered my dad's ashes up there. Being a cyclist, he liked a good hill.

From The Ridgeway one can also see a number of what were in the 1960s to 1980s important centres of nuclear research (The Atomic Energy Research Establishment at Harwell[49] and the Culham Centre for Fusion Energy at Culham, for instance). Being a Communist, my dad liked a good nuclear installation. I suspect he was asked to keep an eye on them. Which brings me to the poem, 'Like Lichen', which not only responds to my sister's interest in such things, but considers the unlikely beauty of faith and of lichen.[50]

Ann Atkinson's poem that follows this is transforming. That use of the word 'hurl' is just brilliant: perfect and mischievous. It is not *about* nature but *of* nature, and as much about human nature as any other, as is Maura Dooley's poem that started this conversation. People, what are we like, always putting ourselves at the centre of the world?

The first of the poems coming up brings us to a stone cottage tucked away up a Welsh valley. I wrote it when I was running away from myself and in a form of hiding. I had come to North Wales, aware that this was the country in which my dad had probably been happiest, to try to be reconciled with my actions.

---

47   What is your favourite prehistoric road?
48   The book, *Middle Ridgeway* by Eric Jones and Patrick Dillon, with paintings by Patrick Dillon's daughter, Anna Dillon, is a fine introduction to this part of the world.
49   Or more accurately the Rutherford Appleton Laboratories.
50   You'll know, from The British Lichen Society's website at www.thebritishlichensociety.org.uk, that lichen is not a single organism but a symbiotic association between a fungus and algae and/or cyanobacteria and that this symbiosis is thought to be a mutualism, since both the fungi and the photosynthetic partners benefit.

And then, having gone back into my father's country of childhood, I go back into mine with two poems about the time before I was myself, when I was just a boy waiting for things to happen. I hope I was bored. There is something magnificent about the boredom of being young. I wish it for every young person.

The poem that closes this section was written in the late 1980s and published in the small magazine, *Staple*. I offer it because I hardly know where it comes from, but it seems to still be alive. I read it as if it is about another person. It probably is.

Just off the A5, West of Llangollen

To swing the gate shut and latch it,
And to begin to walk up the track
Along the cwm, is almost like love.

The stream tilts past you, clattering
The silent heavy air with the crash
And song of tumbling water.

The mud gives way to bare rock, splintered
By seismic pressure, pushed from below:
The life that you have lived, the lies told.

The cottage stands ready; slow, heavy slate
Takes your weight, a small desk,
An old chair. Outside, leaves and hills.

And in the frail, un-leaven moment
You are pulled back into yourself,
Before the fall, the boy; lost, alone.

Note: Cwm: Welsh for valley.

Didcot Parkway

Never Parkway to us
who roamed around
the platforms as boys.

We'd look up the line
to London and see
the nose of a locomotive

seemingly not moving
then suddenly here,
roaring and yellow,

dull blue flanks, its
arrival never as great
as its coming towards us.

Long Hot Summer

Simply this:
the lines of poplars stiff
against the non-existent breeze;

the hours arranged around the fountain
that does not flow
into its pond;

inside the recently creosoted shed
that lost excitement
as we hid;

and on the telephone wires the whistle
of rain abandoning the sky
unconsummated.

The Grass Rash

That we were lost, or that we said
we were lost, goes without saying.
But it is without significance.

But when we lay down on the banks
of an Indian Ocean of Barley
it was the stain of the pigment

of a grass rash on my pallid chest,
showing like a map of the Empire,
irritated pink with possession,

that parted us and put us on the road
to cool my itching skin with water.
We were determined to be self-

determining, to be devolved –
whatever that should mean. And you said
how you would put your top on also

because one is never really alone
up here, just as we may never really
have been together up there, despite

what may or may not have happened.

I have one more of my own poems and then a poem by Sylvia Kantaris, and then, to finish, a brilliantly sombre piece by the German poet Gottfried Benn, translated by Michael Hofmann.

Sylvia Kantaris's poem came to me unexpectedly in a book bought second-hand.[51] I read this collection, *The Sea at the Door*, with little knowledge of what to expect but found myself sharing the poems with others. The poem I feature here, 'After the Birthday', is like nothing I would write myself. It is full of space for understanding.

I came across Gottfried Benn only a few years ago, again by chance. I read up on him – the more than uncomfortable period of history he wrote through; his destructive personal life; his angels and demons. Knowing even a little of this, and of post-war German history, and having myself sat in bars in small German towns, the poem opened up and I was received by it. The poem read me.

I want poems to read me. And I want these poems to read you, to say what you might have said or thought, to be of some use. And I've given this commentary because I want you to know why a small cottage near Llangollen is important to me. Or why bricks are. Or apples.

And while I'm at it, I ask you to take these poems and use them. By which I mean, share them in private correspondence, speak them in your own accent, compose your own – better – versions of them.[52] And if you want to record them as audio files then please do and please send them to me and I'll see if they can't be shared further. The sharing's the thing.

So, to my last poem. It is simple. It is arch and affected. It is pretentious and bombastic. It is short.[53] For these reasons I commend it to you. And then we have Sylvia Kantaris's and Gottfried Benn's, both of which I commend even more.

Thank you for your kind attention.

---

51 I later bought her *Collected Poems*, paying cash to the poet herself.
52 No, really, why ever not?
53 Good.

Quiet the afternoon after rain

Quiet the afternoon after rain
And then the evening leaning back
To observe the coming of night
And then another day is done.

What I fear is not the passing
Of time but how still I find myself
At this point in my life, as if
I know there is nothing I can do.

After The Birthday

By Sylvia Kantaris

... nor questioned since,
Nor cared for corn-flowers wild,
Nor sung with the singing bird.
Christina Rossetti

After the birthday of your life had come
and gone, and you buried the wild corn-flower
and the singing bird deep in your heart,
how was it that you failed to stop their breath?
Why did the flower grow, and grow more blue
in darkness, harbouring untimely seeds,
and why did the imprisoned bird sing
louder still and fill your mouth with music?
The wild things were always too insistent –
and your heart, fuller and more colourful
in autumn than in spring, though resolute –
but then, in winter, so chastised, so bled
and drained of substance for the pale delight
of God that all your wild life suffocated.
And when the bird had stopped its singing
and the flower had lost its sap, pressed flat
between the pages of your prayer-book,
did you still harbour promises of pulse
for pulse and breath for breath in Paradise
on the cold spring birthday of your death?

Listen

By Gottfried Benn, translated by Michael Hofmann

Listen, this is what the last evening will be like
when you're still capable of going out: you're smoking your Junos,
quaffing your three pints of Würzburger Hofbräu
and reading about the UN as reflected in the pages of the *Spiegel*,

you're sitting alone at your little table, the least possible
   company
beside the radiator, because you crave warmth.
All round you mankind and its mewling,
the married couple and their loathsome hound.

That's all you are, you've no house or hill
to call your own, to dream in a sunny landscape,
from your birth to this evening
the walls around you were always pretty tightly drawn.

That's all you were, but Zeus and all the immortals,
the great souls, the cosmos and all the suns
were there for you too, spun and fed through you,
that's all you were, finished as begun –
your last evening – good night.

Gazetteer

Places referenced or pertaining to poems in this collection. Grid references are given where the location is not obvious. All places are in the United Kingdom unless stated otherwise.

Didcot, South Oxfordshire, is my home town. Slightly larger than it used to be what with the new housing estates across the railway, it still has some of its power station and, of course, the railway. The people are generally friendly, it being one of Oxfordshire's less fashionable places.

The River Dee, Llangollen, Denbighshire, is one of the great rivers of North Wales, and into which my mother and a boatload of Lancastrians were accidentally tipped at some point in the late 1950s. They all returned to the riverbank unharmed.

The 'back road' referenced in the poem 'The Back Roads' can be found at 53°01'05.9"N 3°15'30.0"W. It is actually a number of roads, a journey along which would be described by my dad as taking the "back roads". In truth it was a route from a to b involving far too much c, d and e.

The cottage I stayed in when writing 'The Back Roads' is just off the A5, west of Llangollen, at 52°58'27.4"N 3°16'08.8"W. It is close to the village of Glyndyfrdwy and with a track leading up to a hillside of some industry in previous centuries. My thanks to my friend Mindy for allowing me to stay there.

Kurt Schwitters met Edith Thomas at rooms in a building on **St. Stephen's Crescent, Paddington, London.** For Schwitters in the early 1940s, it was better than being interned on the Isle of Man as a suspicious alien. I have no idea if the building still exists and I have no intention of finding out.

Llansannan, Conwy Country Borough, is a small largely Welsh-speaking village to which the Davidson children were evacuated in 1939 to stay with the Joneses.

The Old Main Line Canal (also known as the Birmingham Canal) runs through Smethwick in the West Midlands. The brick in question in the poem 'Utopia' is near 52°29'57.3"N 1°57'34.5"W. The Old Main Line was superseded by the much faster Main Line Canal which had cuttings and fewer locks and was often in a straight line. Over part of both runs an elevated section of the M5. And over us all fly the aeroplanes.

Vilnius, as you will know, is the capital of Lithuania and by some reckoned to be the centre of Europe. Napoleon marched grandly through it on the way to Moscow. On the way back he wasn't so chipper. The annual book fair in Vilnius is extraordinarily popular, with a very large percentage of the Lithuanian population going along.

Miss Balcombe's Orchard, not far from Rowstock, in what was then North Berkshire, is at 51°36'15.0"N 1°19'41.6"W and is now in new ownership. It was a small orchard tended by Miss Balcombe and a temporary workforce of people from local villages and towns, including me and my mum and I think my sister. My dad might have done a few days' work there too. In Miss Balcombe's day (until the 1990s) most of the work was done manually.

A villa (possibly called Villa Marlebäck) in the town of Marlebäck, Finland, was probably where Brecht was photographed playing chess with Margarete Steffin. Mati Unt's novel, *Brecht at Night* seems to bear this out. Brecht and his entourage were staying with Hella Wuolijoki (née Murrick), a progressive Estonian and adopted Finn whose sister, Salme Dutt (née Murrick), was a prominent member of The Communist Party of Great Britain.

Greenham Common Women's Peace Camp around RAF Greenham Common, near Newbury in Berkshire, at 51°22'18.07"N 1°16'40.79"W, was actually a number of camps around the perimeter fence, each with their own methods and style of protest against nuclear weapons. My mum visited on a few occasions and I went once.

Striletska Street 15, Kyiv, Ukraine, is on a winding hill-side street in the old part of Kyiv.

Kyiv Passenger Railway Station, Kyiv, Ukraine, offers direct trains to Moscow, Chisinau, Warsaw and Bucharest as well as Ukrainian destinations. Its main entrance hall is rather magnificent.

Arsenalna Metro Station, Kyiv, Ukraine, is famously deep and doubled as an air-raid shelter in the Soviet period. It is named after the old city arsenal building above it, now the venue for the annual Book Arsenal (book fair and festival).

The Ridgeway is along the Oxfordshire/Berkshire border, for instance at 51°33'19.8"N 1°19'05.6"W. This is close to my ancestral home, with good views towards Oxford. The steep scarp slope faces north; behind that the dip slope falls gently towards the River Kennet.

Padley Woods, Hope Valley, Derbyshire is at 53°18'26.7"N 1°37'24.2"W and is just up from Grindleford Station (on the line from Sheffield to Manchester) and not far from where Ann Atkinson used to live. The nearby Companion Stones includes one with a poem by Ann carved into it, www.companionstones.org.

Didcot Parkway Station, Didcot, Oxfordshire, is on the railway line originally laid out by Isambard Kingdom Brunel between London and Bristol, and the junction for the line north to Oxford. The whole line is fast, but from here to Swindon it's a racetrack.

Bibliography

Books, magazines & other ephemera pertaining to poems in this collection.

The Singing & the Dancing, Ann Atkinson, Smith|Doorstop, 2015

Impromptus: Selected Poems, Gottfried Benn, translated by Michael Hofmann, Faber & Faber, 2014

Love Poems, Bertolt Brecht, translated by David Constantine, Tom Kuhn and Barbara Brecht Schall, Liveright, 2015

Brick Building in Britain, R W Brunskill, Victor Gollancz Ltd, 1990

Settlements, Catherine Byron, Taxus Press, 1985

Marilyn Monroe and other poems, Ernesto Cardenal, translated by Robert Pring-Mill, Search Press, 1975

The Living Room, Jonathan Davidson, Arc Publications, 1994

Early Train, Jonathan Davidson, Smith|Doorstop, 2011

Humfrey Coningsby: poems, complaints, explanations and demands for satisfaction, Jonathan Davidson, Valley Press, 2014

On Poetry, Jonathan Davidson, Smith|Doorstop, 2018

Poems, Walter de la Mare, Penguin Books Ltd, 1962

Middle Ridgeway, Eric Jones and Patrick Dillon, Paintings by Anna Dillon, Wessex Books, 2016

Sound Barrier, Poems 1982-2002, Maura Dooley, Bloodaxe Books, 2002

How Equal Temperament Ruined Harmony (and Why You Should Care), Ross W. Duffin, WW Norton and Company Inc, New York, 2008

Counting Backwards: Poems 1975-2017, Helen Dunmore, Bloodaxe Books, 2019

How to Dismantle a Hotel Room, Roz Goddard, Coal Press Publishing, 2006

New Collected Poems, W S Graham, edited by Matthew Francis, Faber & Faber, 2005

Poet and Critic: The Letters of Ted Hughes and Keith Sagar, The British Library Publishing Division, 2012

Dirty Washing: New & Selected Poems, Sylvia Kantaris, Bloodaxe Books, 1989

Darling: New & Selected Poems, Jackie Kay, Bloodaxe Books, 2007

British Bricks, David Kitching, Amberley Publishing, 2016

Us, Zaffar Kunial, Faber & Faber, 2018

The Whitsun Weddings, Philip Larkin, Faber & Faber, 1964

Passport, Richie McCaffery, Nine Arches Press, 2018

Map: Poems After William Smith's Geological Map of 1815, edited by. Michael McKimm, Worple Press, 2015

The Tree Line: Poems for Trees, Woods and People, edited by Michael McKimm, Worple Press, 2017

Staple, Winter 1990-91, Staple Magazine, edited by Donald Measham & Bob Windsor, 1991

Why Brownlee Left, Paul Muldoon, Faber & Faber, 1980

The Pheasant Plucker's Son, Mick North, Littlewood + Arc, 1990

Cantus in Memoriam Benjamin Britten, Arvo Pärt, 1977, various recordings available.

A Little Larger than the Entire Universe: Selected Poems, Fernando Pessoa, translated by Richard Zenith, Penguin Classics, 2006

On Playing the Flute, Johann Joachim Quantz, translated by Edward R Reilly, Faber & Faber, 2001

The Leveller Revolution, John Rees, Verso, 2016

The Honeycomb, Pauline Stainer, Bloodaxe Books, 1989

Brecht at Night, Mati Unt, translated by Eric Dickens, Dalkey Archive Press, 2009

Hoping it might be so: poems 1974-2000, Kit Wright, Leviathan, 2000

Ode to Didcot Power Station, Kit Wright, Bloodaxe, 2014

Solid Geology Map, UK South Sheet, 1:625,000 Scale, 4th Edition, British Geological Survey

Acknowledgements

My thanks to the International Writers' and Translators' House at Ventspils, Latvia, where some of this book was written. A number of poems were first published in *Antiphon Poetry Magazine, Culture and Change* (British Council Ukraine, 2017), *Early Train* (Smith|Doorstop, 2011), *The Everyday Poet* (Michael O'Mara Books, 2016), *The Fenland Reed, The Living Room* (Arc Publications, 1994), *Map: Poems After William Smith's Geological Map of 1815* (Worple Press, 2015), *Staple Magazine, The Tree Line: Poems for Trees, Woods & People* (Worple Press, 2017).

'The Silence' was awarded 1st Prize in the 2013 BBC Proms Poetry Competition. 'Brickwork' won 1st Prize in the 2014 Café Writers Open Poetry Competition. 'A Quadratic Equation' won 2nd Prize in 2018 Charles Causley International Poetry Competition. 'Clouding Over' was longlisted for the Candlestick Press 2017 Cloud Poetry Competition.

I am grateful to the following for permission to reprint poems: Arc Publications for 'Land' by Mick North; Catherine Byron for her poem 'Night Flight to Belfast'; Roz Goddard for her poem 'Winter, Lye Waste'; Nine Arches Press for 'Bricks' by Richie McCaffery; Kit Wright for his poem 'Sonnet for Dick'; Zaffar Kunial for his poem 'The Lyric Eye'; Sylvia Kantaris for her poem 'After the Birthday'; Bloodaxe Books for 'The Honeycomb' by Pauline Stainer, 'Six Filled the Woodshed with Soft Cries' by Maura Dooley, 'Darling' by Jackie Kay; Faber & Faber for 'Listen' by Gottfried Benn (translated by Michael Hofmann).

I am grateful to the many people who have read and responded to various drafts of this book, including Jo Bell, Liz Berry, Alison Brackenbury, Robbie Burton, Catherine Byron, Anne Caldwell, Natasha Carlish, Paul Casey, Olivia Chapman, Jane Commane, David Clarke, Andy Croft, Cahal Dallet, Sylvia Davidson, Anna Drada, Sasha Dugdale, Pat Edwards, Anne-Marie Fyfe, Roz Goddard, Matt

Holland, Nadia Kingsley, Gregory Leadbetter, Richie McCaffery, Kim Moore, Lisa Peter and Simon Thirsk. I am grateful to *The Zellig Group*, the members of which have responded to many of these poems, and to Lisa Peter and Liv Chapman for marketing and project management support.

I am grateful to Anna Dillon, for permission to use the cover image, from her painting 'The Industrial Henge'. More details of her work can be found on www.annadillon.com

ON POETRY

JONATHAN DAVIDSON

'From attentive close readings to thoughts of how poems might best be shared, his belief in poetry and its ability to touch and transform us shines throughout. This small book is a gem and any reader interested in poetry and how it can enrich our lives will find Davidson a fine companion.'
– Liz Berry

'Wonderfully diverting, affably anecdotal, and profoundly readable ... Davidson is a great leveller, rightly asserting that poetry is for everyone.'
– The Yorkshire Times

'The best thing about Davidson as a critic is that he isn't distracted in his quest to find the real deal. What interests him is 'what remains when the fuss has died down—the quiet voices' ... This is a book, refreshingly, not for the academic, though academics might enjoy it, but for the writers. And, of course the listeners.'
– London Grip

'I found much to reward and contemplate in Jonathan Davidson's *On Poetry*'
– Jane Commane, Nine Arches Press

*

ISBN 978-1-910367-93-3 | £9.95
poetrybusiness.co.uk/product/on-poetry
Receive 20% off with code: JDAC20%

smith|doorstop

EARLY TRAIN

JONATHAN DAVIDSON

'Jonathan Davidson has a loving, observant and wry regard for the frailties of the human condition. He makes fresh something we thought we knew; writing of the everyday the way Vermeer might be said to paint it.'
— Maura Dooley

'These are thoughtful, lucid, deceptively simple poems; but their eye is clear and their approach graceful. Sometimes concealing a darker melancholy, they find truths in the prosaic details of our lives – such as bike frames and Sunday papers in the garden.'
— Stuart Maconie

'Distant and yet close, intimate and yet somehow objective, the quiet power of these tender and true poems pulls you in. Davidson is as interested in the haunting strangeness of nostalgia as he is in the oddly humanising effect of the mundane. And he often finds in the ordinary something joyous and surprising. This is a remarkable collection.'
— Jackie Kay

'These poems are carefully crafted, even artful, almost exquisite at times in the ways they precisely deploy the language of the everyday and images of ordinariness. Davidson documents the personal importance of everyday things in such a way that what might be thought trivial is discovered to be essential, and what might be ignored as commonplace finds it own voice.'
— Orbis

*

ISBN 978-1-906613-3-27 | £9.95
poetrybusiness.co.uk/product/early-train

smith|doorstop

A COMMONPLACE

JONATHAN DAVIDSON

Praise for *A Commonplace*

'This book and its poems are very good, in brave
and unusual ways.'
– Alison Brackenbury

'*A Commonplace* is hugely readable – original, modest,
wise and entertaining (the chatty footnotes work espe-
cially well). Above all, it is a friendly book, an invitation
to join a conversation, not a lecture or an intellectual
ultimatum.'
– Andy Croft, Smokestack Books

'What shines through is the openness of the venture and
the sense of poetic community and involvement of different voices and poetics in a constant communion.'
– Sasha Dugdale

*

ISBN 978-1-912196-33-3 | £9.95
poetrybusiness.co.uk/product/a-commonplace
smith|doorstop